Why Christians Believe

Why Christians Believe

Understanding the reasons why anyone would decide to become a Christian

by

Dave Powers

Harvest Publishing
Newport Beach, California

Why Christians Believe
Copyright 2007 by Dave Powers
ISBN 978-0-6151-7810-3

Harvest Publishing, Newport Beach,California

All Scripture quotations, unless otherwise noted, are taken from the Holy Bible: New International Version (North American Edition). Copyright 1973, 1978, 1984 by International Bible Society. Used by permission of Zondervan. All rights reserved

The "NIV" and "New International Version" trademarks are registered in the United States Patent and Trademark Office by International Society

All rights reserved. No part of this publication may be reproduced, stored in a retrieval system, or transmitted in any form or by any means – electronic, mechanical, photocopy, recording, or any other – except for brief quotations in printed reviews, without prior permission of the publisher.

Dedicated to my wife Jenny and our family, who have helped me in each step of my journey to believing.

Contents

Introduction

For the past 2000 years, millions upon millions of people from around the world have committed their lives to the person of Jesus Christ. Often times to the bewilderment of friends and families who wonder, *why*. Why would anyone believe in this Person, in the claims that He made, in the promises that He made? And for those who do believe, there is often a struggle to find the right words to adequately explain the *reasons* for their belief's, to the people they care about.

Why Christians Believe is not intended to be a defense of Christianity. In these next few short pages, the intention is solely to help define some of the reasons why a person, any person would put their trust in the person of Jesus Christ. This book does not address the vast number of doctrinal issues associated with Christian beliefs. Its focus will be on a limited amount of the vast evidences available to substantiate a person's decision to becoming a follower of Jesus Christ. And in the process, hopefully, to help Believers become better equipped in explaining to others their reasons for believing. And for those who have not yet come to belief, some grounds for better understanding their friends and family. And perhaps even to aid in their own journey to believing in this incredible person called Jesus.

Chapter One

A Simple Beginning

One of the basics beliefs of the Christian faith is God. Christianity, simply put, believes God exists. And God is a personal Being who has a genuine interest not only in all of "humankind", but in each and every individual person on this planet. Not only did He create us, but He has gone to great lengths in order to reestablish a relationship with us, a relationship which we severed by our own defiant willfulness. And His primary means of reestablishing that relationship is in the person of Jesus Christ.

Most often we hear Christians say, "I believe in God, because I have Him in my heart." And as good as that is, all too often Christians have resorted to this as the only "evidence" needed. One of the reasons for this is because we just don't want to do the thinking that's needed to provide the evidence upon which to base that belief.

Several years ago a friend told me, "You know Dave, you believe what you believe because you grew up in church. And your background has tainted your thinking." And they are partly right. My upbringing has a very strong influence on what I think. As is true of anyone, regardless of whether we were raised "in church" or not. But I hope, that over the years, I have become enough of my own person to be able to think through, what I believe about things.

I have to admit, that even among Christians, there are many different "beliefs". And with any given group of Believers there are vast differences in the beliefs regarding God. But even with all the differences Christians have, there is also a shared belief in the person of God.

When the question is raised, "Is there a God?" We are presented with 3 options: 1. No 2. Maybe and 3. Yes. Those are the choices for anyone investigating this issue. But where do those choices lead us?

To say "No" God doesn't exist, we have to ask, "What's the evidence?" Now it's true that Christians often get lazy in their thinking and reasoning. It's also true of those of us who say, "I just know there is no God." That's a pretty big statement. I mean to know, with absolute certainty that there is no God means we would have to be conscience of every planet, of every dimension of time and space, of everything that exists period. We would have to be, "all knowing." If any of us ask, where is the proof that God exists, so we must ask for the proof that He doesn't.

When the Russian cosmonaut Yuri Gagarin returned from orbiting earth in 1961, he is quoted as having said, *"I didn't see God out there."* Is that sufficient evidence? If we can't physically see, physically touch, smell or literally hear God, then He must not exist, right? Is this the only reliable source for knowing of God's existence? Are our senses alone sufficient to substantiate the existence of God?

We could take the position of "Maybe". He may exist, but does anyone really know? But again, this is quite similar to saying God does not exist. Since God is not perceived by our five senses, we are limited in how much we can know about God. What we really need is sufficient evidence – not absolute evidence.

And that leads us to the "Yes" answer. So you may be thinking, "Alright Dave, you wrote this book, what evidence did you base your decision on?" There are several evidences which point to a personal God. Three specific evidences that deserve our investigation:

What You See - Is What You Get

The existence of matter, points to the existence of God (Cosmological Evidence). The very existence of matter, of a universe points to the hand of a Creator. There has been a great deal of confusion on this issue. Often due to arguments that have long since been refuted.

Take for example the thought that creation is simply the result of an infinite amount of time and an infinite supply of matter and that over an infinite amount of time, through a process of purely random order, there began to form atoms, then cells, then a strain of DNA and eventually life as we know it.

Immanual Kant, who lived in the 17th Century, was one of the first to put forth the idea of an infinitely old and infinitely large universe. And according to Kant's reasoning, an infinitely old and infinitely large universe would permit an infinite number of random opportunities for life to originate. Thus even such highly improbable events as; atoms self-assembling into human beings might be possible. Now Kant was a believer in God. But the science of his day perpetuated the idea that the universe was infinite, that time was infinite and there existed an infinite supply of matter from which to build the universe. So in order for "faith" not to look foolish in light of "science" Kant formulated these ideas.

But Kant's philosophical approach was based on faulty information. We have long since discovered that we live in a finite universe, a finite measure of time and that there is a finite number of atoms, molecules and matter available. So the ideas of Kant and others who suggest that the universe and our world were created solely by chance, are questionable. It's questioned because of several discoveries made primarily in the last 100 years. There are several discoveries that have helped refute a "random" world.

The first is a discovery Albert Einstein made in 1905. Although most of us are not mathematicians, if I were to ask, "What is Einstein's great discovery?" Most of us could finish this equation: E = MC? Einstein's theory of relativity, which is $E=MC^2$. This formula has been used as the premise in a number of scientific discoveries. Part of Einstein's theory, is that everything in the universe is simultaneously expanding and decelerating. Now, if the universe is in the process of expansion and decelaration, then sometime in its past there must have been a beginning. A point in time when all that exists came into existence.

At first Mr. Einstein was unwilling to acknowledge the idea that the universe had a beginning. However, in 1929, a new discovery brought new information to light. In 1929, Edwin Hubble proved that galaxies were in fact moving away from one another in the very manner predicted by Einstein's formula of relativity. Confronted with this new knowledge, Mr. Einstein gave in to the necessity for a beginning, and to "the presence of a superior reasoning power".

But there is a second reason why the cosmological evidence points to the existence of the person of God. This evidence came to light on April 24, 1992. This discovery was on the front page of leading newspapers around the world. This discovery was so vast that Ted Koppel began his TV show Nightline, in which he interviewed astronomers and astrophysicist's, by quoting the first two verses of the first chapter of the book of Genesis.

So what was this incredible discovery? On April 24, 1992 the Cosmic Background Explorer (COBE) sent back measurements of the temperature of the universe. As one news reporter stated, "COBE has in essence taken the universe's temperature." And through that measurement scientist have concluded as George Smoot at the University of California at Berkeley stated, *"We have found the evidence for the birth of the universe."*

This discovery did in fact substantiate a beginning of the universe, and more specifically, the origin of the universe. COBE's discovery was so significant that many in the science community have been rethinking their ideas regarding our origin and the beginning of our universe. But COBE is only one of the discoveries that have had this kind of impact for rethinking our existence.

More and more the scientific research of our day is pointing to a Beginning. Now you may be thinking, "We hear about these outrageous discoveries and the scientific research, but who can measure the universe? How can anyone on this planet tell that the universe is expanding?" Allow me to bring this closer to home.

Take a simple 18cm Ruler. (Go ahead, find one, I'll wait.) The first 6cm on that ruler measures the distance the moon has moved away from the earth since this time last year. The first 12cm measures the distance the moon has moved over the past 2 years. And the overall length of 18cm measures the distance the moon has moved away from the earth in only the past 3 years. These measurements were made by a means most of us are familiar with: micro waves. Any fisherman who has ever used a fish finder knows the principle. A signal is sent into the water and bounces back and tells you exactly where the fish are located. Well, they set up a giant fish finder in the desert and measured exactly how far the moon is traveling from the earth. OK, maybe it's a little more complicated than that, but it is definitely a process most of us are quite familiar with. This measurement is in fact, only one of the many evidences that the universe is expanding. And if the universe is expanding, it had a beginning.

Whether it be Einstein's formula, or the discovery of the COBE satellite, or a flood of other recent discoveries, they are all pointing to an undeniable fact: There was a point in time when everything that we see, everything that exists – did not. There was a time when there was no time, when there was no light, when there was no matter. Then, there was a time, when time, light and matter began.

In 1970 three British astrophysicists: Stephen Hawking, George Ellis, and Roger Penrose did extensive research on Einstein's theory of relativity. Primarily to test its validity. To the best of my knowledge none of these men have ever claimed to be "Christians" or "believers'. But they did make some very interesting conclusions. One of their conclusions was that Einstein's formula was, in fact, valid and correct. Stephen Hawking writes in his conclusion, "Time its self must have a beginning."

The good news is this, if there is a beginning, then there is a Beginner. Someone who called everything into existence. The greater news is we can know the One who called time and light and matter into being. Not just a "force" in the universe, but a Heavenly Father. Someone who not only called us into being, but also gives us purpose every day of our life on this small little dot in space.

Now does the Cosmological Evidence give us absolute evidence of the existence of God? Not at all. If that were the only evidence we had, I would be among the first to say there are reasons to question God's existence. But that leads to our second piece of evidence.

Intentional Design

The design of our world points to the Designer (Teleological Evidence). The word *telos* in Greek means – The End. This approach of study originated with the Greeks who came to this conclusion: That the way things operate (what they do) tells us why they exist. The Greeks concluded centuries ago, there is a unique design, an order to things in the universe, on this planet and even in our own lives. And the order of things points to, does not provide absolute evidence, but points to a purpose for the existence of things, including us.

Teleology is the view that the universe is designed for a purpose, for intention. And this intention can be seen in the world around us. Now it's true many people have a difficult time seeing there is a purpose to all that we see. But this design, this intention, does point to something. We could look at the universe and conclude everything is here by accident. Or we could look for the evidence that the very nature of things proves otherwise.

Take for example this little sphere we are riding on. This *Pale Blue Dot* Dr. Carl Sagan referred to. Scientists tell us if this little blue dot, were only 10% larger or smaller, life as we know it could not exist here. That small difference makes a huge difference in who, or what, inhabits this earth. In addition, no other planet in the universe is on a 23.5 degree axis tilt. This slight tilt, allows for equal warming and cooling of both the northern and southern hemispheres. A tilt held in place by our moon.

And the next time we're sitting in the backyard and we look up to the moon, remember something: Without the moon, the craters we see there, would have been here, destroying life on this planet. In addition, without the moon, we have no ocean tides. The slow methodical ebb and flow of the ocean tides, that literally washes the earth. Without ocean tides we have no waves breaking upon the shores, aerating the water which feeds the plankton, which is the basic foundation to the food chain on this planet.

Then there is the atmosphere itself; 78% nitrogen, 21% oxygen and 1% trace elements. No other planet in the known universe has the composition such as this. And these elements are not chemically combined, they are mechanically combined by the effect of the moon's gravitational pull upon the atmosphere. This unique pull the moon has upon the earth is essential for the earth being the place of inhabitance for people.

Then there is the process of cycling nitrogen into the soil. Nitrogen is extremely inert. If that were not so, we would all be dead from nitrogen poisoning. However, because of its inertness, it is virtually impossible for us to get it to combine with other materials. And yet nitrogen is an essential element for plant life and for the existence of man and beast. So how does nitrogen find its way into the soil? Lightening! 100,000 lightening bolts strike this planet every day. And as best as scientists can measure, this creates around 100 million tons of usable nitrogen plant food every year. What's the primary source for conveying lightening? Thunderstorms! Those annoying, sometimes frightening claps of thunder following a flash of lightening in the sky, are part of the system to keep the earth producing food and life.

But thunderstorms do more than just deliver lightening. They deliver life giving water. Through the process of falling rain, this unique solvent dissolves almost everything on this planet except those things that are life-sustaining. This amazing liquid breaks up rock, which in turn produces soils, which in turn fertilizes the land, which in turn produces food. Water exists in the form of ice, in snow, in liquid and in vapor form. Each form having their own specific function to fulfill in order to sustain life on earth.

Even that annoying, sneeze producing particle called dust has a purpose. If it were not for dust, we would never see a blue sky. Seventeen miles above the earth surface, there is no dust and therefore the sky is black. Dust is necessary in order to collect water vapor, thus producing the blue skies we enjoy. And dust is even necessary for producing rain. One drop of rain is made up of eight million droplets of water, all of which are wrapped around a single tiny particle of dust. Without dust it would never rain.

Then there's the order of things inside of every one of us. Take for example the red blood cell found in the human body. It's created in the bone marrow, but upon reaching the bloodstream it immediately gives up its nucleus. It is the only cell in the human body to function like this. Then without the nucleus, the blood cell takes on a donut shape. Whereupon it builds a thin membrane across the space the nucleus left empty. This shape and this membrane, allows the cell to carry more oxygen throughout the body. If it were shaped like other cells, it would require nine times more blood cells to provide oxygen to our bodies.

So every time we look into the sky, every time we watch the waves crash on the shore, every time we watch the moon rise full in the evening, or the sun come up right on schedule in the morning, we are reminded there is an order to things. The *telos* points not only to a Creator, but to the Creator who called all these things together for a purpose.

Again we must ask, is this order of things absolute evidence on the existence of God? No! But to these two pieces of this puzzle that reveals the reality of God, we add a third.

We Are Wonderfully Made

Who we are, points to a personal God (Anthropological Evidence). If we look to ourselves for just a moment, who we are; with our intellect, our emotions, our personality, with our talents and abilities, all of which points to a

Creator who made us – us! And the old saying is true, "It takes all kinds of people to make up this world." You and I are just one of many "ones" that have been made different than everyone else. Therein are more evidences that call our attention to a Personal Creator:

We Think About Things

We would have to acknowledge we are more than electrochemical process of mental thought. Our thoughts go beyond just the process of filtering information through our brain. We reflect upon abstract issues. Things like justice, wisdom, beauty and even our existence. As one philosopher said: "We not only think about the future, but we think about the process of thinking about the future."

The uniqueness of who we are, that somehow we are not identical models of those who came before us, speaks to a unique creation. No one on this planet thinks like you and I think. Many have thoughts similar to ours, but each person's thoughts are unique. There are things we agree about politically, economically and socially. But no one thinks "identically" to another person. And this uniqueness directs us to a unique origin. Then there is the fact:

We Enjoy The Beauty Of Creation

It is true that beauty is in the eye of the beholder. But there have been times for all of us when we have viewed what someone has made and saw it's beauty. We may not even be very "artsy" but we can see the beauty in what was once simply a slab of marble, then fashioned into a statue. Or the colors placed skillfully on a canvas by someone who had the gift of painting. And while there may be huge differences in what we call beauty, there is, at the same time a huge consensus concerning the beauty that can be enjoyed in art, or in music, or in literature. This awareness cannot be reduced to a mechanical response to sensory input. This capacity to enjoy the gift of others transcends the material world. It is truly a gift of our Creator. But there is a third evidence in mankind:

We Have A Sense Of Morality

From the beginning of time, people have sought an answer to "Why am I here? What should I do?" Now it is true that there are times we have worshipped rocks, the birds, the moon and even ourselves. But there has always been a hungering in the hearts of humankind to have a higher authority. Even in the sense of setting standards for ourselves. Our sense of morality is a universal human experience. Although there are variations, qualities like honesty, wisdom, courage and fairness continue to be regarded as virtues across cultural lines. Even if a person holds to the idea that morals are the result of cultural conditioning, he shows himself to be just like all of us when he criticizes or praises another for their actions or efforts. Even our sense of right and wrong, speaks to us about a Creator.

The world around us and even our own existence points to something beyond us. And while it does not provide "absolute" evidence of God, it does raise enough of a question that it is well within reason to ask, "How did we get here, and why are we here?" Ultimately this evidence has led many people to conclude that "how" we got here, has much to do with "why" we are here. That our beginning has much to do with our Beginner.

Recently the History Channel showed a series of programs regarding the origin of the universe. The final program in the series interviews several scientists regarding the Big Rip theory. The Big Rip Theory has to do with the end of our universe. Basically, that as the universe continues to expand, it will one day reach a point that it will tear itself apart. Causing planets to explode and causing everything to destroy itself, even down to an atomic level. Now the good news is it will take another five billion years to reach that point, so we have a little time.

But long before the end of the universe, we will all be gone. Our life on this Pale Blue Dot lasts only so long. And that reality raises the question that only each of us can answer for ourselves, "If there is a Beginner, a Creator, who made me, why was I made? Does my Creator have any expectations of me? How can I know what those expectations are?" Questions that are well worth the asking.

Chapter Two

A Reliable Source

There has been a source of insight people have referred to for thousands of years. The beliefs of Christians are found primarily in the book we most often refer to as The Bible. For our purpose of study, we will refer to the Bible as any standard translation in existence today, such as the New International Version, or the American Standard Bible, or even the old King James Version, whose translation has been the result of a variety of scholars from a diversity of backgrounds working together to complete such an effort. This would preclude any "special" translations such as the Book of Mormon Bible, or the Jehovah Witness Bible or a variety of smaller religious groups that must have their "Own" version in order to protect a doctrine or teaching.

The Bible is the most unusual book that has ever been printed and the first book to ever be put into modern print. It was written over fifteen hundred years; by forty different authors; in three different languages; over forty generations. No other book, religious or otherwise, even comes close to the unique characteristics of the Bible. For the longest time those who have rejected the Bible, have taken a position that the Bible is simply man's attempt to define God. But Christians have taken a position throughout the years that the Bible is God's effort to reach out to us, to care for mankind.

So why do Christians believe that? What evidence is there to substantiate that the Bible is trustworthy, that its message can be relied upon? There are three evidences:

1. The Bible Has Told Us The Truth About Our Universe

One of the criticisms of the Bible is that it is out of touch with reality. It is behind the times and science is miles ahead of the Bible. But let's look at the evidence. There is an amazing amount of scientific fact in the Bible. Facts the Bible was teaching about our universe long before it was scientifically recognized. For example:

A. Until 1492 the scientific community taught that the world was a flat disk. But long before that discovery was ever made, the Bible taught that the Earth is a sphere. In Isaiah. 40:22 we read, *"He sits enthroned above the circle of the earth . . ."* What do we know today – that the Earth is a sphere

B. Until discoveries as recent as 1929, science has taught that the number of stars totaled somewhere around 1,100. But long before the Hubble's discovery in 1929, the Bible taught that number of stars where in the billions. In Jeremiah 33:22 we read, *"I will make the descendants of David my servant and the Levites who minister before me as countless as the stars of the sky and as measureless as the sand on the seashore."* What do we know today about the stars in the heavens: They number in the billions.

C. Until the 17th Century science held firm that all stars in the heavens were the same. But long before it was scientifically accepted, the Bible taught that every star is different. In I Corinthians 15:41we read, *"The sun has one kind of splendor, the moon another and the stars another; and star differs from star in splendor."* What do we know today: That in fact every star is different.

There is a long list of science *fact* the Bible has taught before it was ever accepted as fact in the scientific community. But the Bible has told us even more.

2. The Bible Has Told Us The Truth About Our Past
For years the criticism regarding the Bible telling us about our past has been two-fold.
A. Either the prophecies found in the Old Testament are so ambiguous or so generic they could be fulfilled in a number of different ways. Or,
B. The Bible has been "rewritten" a number of times along the way so that the prophecies can match up with history.

There's a little "fact" we need to be reminded. Find a Bible real quick. (It's OK, I'll wait again.) Now go to those few pages that typically separate the Old Testament from the New Testament. As you look at the two divisions of the Bible, the section you have on the left, the Old Testament, was translated from the Hebrew into Greek in about 250 BC. During the reign of Ptolemy II Philadelphus. This translation from Hebrew to the Greek, is referred to as the "Septuagint". The Septuagint was in print, was being read and was being used to teach, 250 years before Christ was born. And one of the ways we know this to be true is because of the Dead Sea Scrolls.

Now we hear a lot about the Dead Sea Scrolls and how they have disproved or in some way compromised the Bible we have today. It's amazing to me the amount of *talk* that goes around about things that really aren't substantiated with fact. So I took the liberty of sitting down and reading the Translation of the Dead Sea Scrolls. Not so that I would in some way impress anyone, but rather so when someone says, "I hear the Dead Sea Scrolls just tears up the Bible." There is a reasonable response that can be made. A response of, "Have you read the Dead Sea Scrolls? Well I know this Pastor that did. You know what he discovered?"

A. There is no contradiction in any part of the texts of scripture of any part of the Old Testament. And, in no way does the Dead Seas Scrolls compromise our present day translation of the Old Testament and

B. What we are reading today is what people were reading 250 years before Christ was born. And that the prophesies we find in the Old Testament we are reading today, were in print and verifiable 250 years before Christ was born.

This is a very important historical fact. Because we often hear someone say, "the prophecies of the Bible have been manipulated so that they match the outcome." The catch is this: The Old Testament has been around longer than the fulfillment of the prophecies. Let's look at a couple, take for example the Hittites. The Hittites are found in several different Old Testament passages of scripture, including: Genesis 15:19, 23:3, 49:32, Exodus 3:8. 13:15, 23:27, 34:11, and I Kings 9:20. The Bible tells us that the Hittites were a "Super Power" in the ancient world.

On a number of occasions the Israelites had contact with the Hittites, and on some occasions even went to battle against them. But, for the longest time the archaeological community claimed this was proof of how confused the Bible is. According to archaeology, the Hittites never existed. And if they ever did exist, they were probably some small nomadic tribe, hardly to be considered a "Super Power" in the ancient world.

From the beginning of the study of archaeology in about 1800, this *fact* of no evidence of the Hittites only helped prove that the Bible was wrong. And if the Bible was wrong about the Hittites, it must be wrong about a lot of things, was the reasoning of the day.

Take a quick trip to, www.thehistorychannel.com and type in "Hittites". (Go ahead, I'll wait again.) There we find that archaeologist have long since acknowledged that the Hittites were in fact one of the most powerful nations in the ancient world. It wasn't until 1906 that Dr Hugo Winckler made the discovery of the Hittite nation. He further discovered that not only were the Hittites strong enough to have built forty different cities, but for about five hundred years they were so powerful, that the Babylonians and the Egyptians may very well have been only tribes of the Hittite nation.

But this also addresses what a lot of people have heard: That the Bible has been rewritten to accommodate the Prophecies in the Old Testament. If that were the case, who ever was rewriting the Bible in 1800, should have taken the Hittites out, because they were an embarrassment to the Bible. Instead those prophecies remained, and what the Bible claimed as fact, took archaeologist hundreds of years to finally reveal as such.

Take for example the city of Babylon. The History Channel tells us that the Babylonians came into power about 1750 BC. And at the heart of the Babylonian Empire was the great city of Babylon. Her defense was a marvel to the world at that time. She had a set of double walls, two hundred feet high, with watch towers three hundred and thirty feet high that stretched for fifteen miles, and encompassed one hundred and ninety six square miles of the city. Within the city of Babylon were the famous *Hanging Gardens*, considered one of the Seven Wonders of the World. Yet at her zenith, when Babylon was at its strongest point, Isaiah the prophet who lived in 750 BC made a prophecy, "Babylon is going to fall." (Isaiah 13)

Let's remember this was in a time in history when we didn't have the ability to look back and see the rise and fall of the great empires in history. The city of Babylon was impenetrable. There are over a hundred prophecies about the fall of the Babylon Empire. Jeremiah the prophet, who lived in 627 BC, went so far as to say in Jeremiah 51, that not only would the city fall, but that it would be uninhabited. This went contrary to the thinking of the day because even then historians knew that once a city fell, it could and probably would be reinhabited some time in the future.

For over two hundred years Isaiah's prophecy regarding the Fall of Babylon was laughed at. Then, came Cyrus the Great of Persia. Who in 539 BC, came to town with an idea: "I'll defeat the Babylonians, and take over the city of Babylon." And guess what happened? He did exactly what Isaiah said would happen, two hundred years earlier. Not only did Cyrus the Great defeat the Babylonians, but he conquered the great city of Babylon.

But Jeremiah said the city would be uninhabited. Cyrus had left the walls intact. Onto the scene comes Alexander the Great in 333 BC. Alexander tried to rebuild the city, but shortly after giving the orders he died and the work stopped. Although Babylon never became a great city, it remained inhabited until the 4th century AD. When the Roman general Julian the Apostate, defeated the Persians and dismantled the walls to the city of Babylon. The Great Wall of China, which predates Babylon, still stands, but to this day Babylon is a wasteland. No one lives there.

But it's not just history that's prophesied about in the Old Testament. The Old Testament goes so far as to tell us about the Messiah. Let's remember that the Old Testament was in print two hundred and fifty years before Christ was born. And the Dead Sea Scrolls have helped determine that what we are reading today was what was written nearly 3000 years ago.

There are more than three hundred Old Testament prophecies regarding the Messiah, and His coming into the world. Of the three hundred, there are what scholars refer to as the 60 major prophecies.

These 60 Major Prophecies include the Tribe He will be a part of, the manner of his birth, the place of His birth, the manner of His death and specific details surrounding His death and even a time line when He would begin his public ministry. As we go even further into the 60 Major Prophecies, we discover they become even more exact about events regarding the Messiah.

Even if we wanted to dismiss the; born of a virgin, born in Bethlehem, prophecies; we must still contend with the fact the Romans, did in fact place a crown of thrones, did in fact pierce His hands and feet, did in fact gamble for His garments, did in fact run a spear into His side. All of these are events that none of His followers could have orchestrated. When we talk about the Old Testament and all of its prophecies, it leads us point blank to the New Testament and to a question: Were all these prophecies fulfilled by a person named Jesus? Which brings us to the last reason why the Bible can be trusted.

3. It Tells Us The Truth About Ourselves

From one end of the book to the other we keep finding, ourselves. Take for example the time Jesus was talking to a crowd of people. A crowd of people with worries and fears and cares just like any of us, and as recorded in Matthew 11:28, He said, *"Come to me, all you who are weary and burdened and I will give you rest."* Suddenly we begin to realize the Bible moves beyond scientific and archaeological thinking and it begins to address a greater need. The need of every human being on this planet to know there is a God who cares. A God, who knows our fears, our worries, even our struggle with sin and says, "I want to give you rest"

In 1850 there was a very noted archaeologist named Sir William Ramsay. He was an atheist and the son of an atheist. He was wealthy and had his Ph.D. from Oxford. Somewhere along the line he had read the book of Acts, and came to the conclusion that he would go to Palestine and not only refute the Book of Acts but disprove the Bible. So he went and he studied. The more he studied, the more he began to realize the Bible is more than fact and history.

After writing several research studies, books that became a foundation for archaeological study. Sir Ramsay eventually wrote a book, in which he acknowledged that after all his investigations, after all of his research and archaeological digs, he was becoming a Christian. Now this really shocked the archaeological community. Sir Ramsey was the Defender of Intelellect. But Sir Ramsay had come to terms with not just the history of the Book, but the person of the Book – the person of Jesus Christ.

Several years ago I came across a copy of his last book, entitled, *St Paul The Traveller and The Roman Citizen,* printed in 1895. As I read through Sir Ramsey's last work, I could see a man who needed fact, he needed evidence. Sir Ramsay was a man who needed to *know* what he believed. And he found his evidence. But he was also a man who found great truth in Psalm 34: *"I cried out to the Lord in my suffering and He heard me. He set me free from all my fears."*

What person when reading Jeremiah 29:11; *"For I know the plans I have for you says the Lord, plans to prosper you and not to harm you, plans to give you a hope and a future.",* doesn't have hope rise up within them. A hope, that if there were a Creator, the Creator of everything that exists would be interested in each of us. That He would sit on high and be mindful of our struggles. And not only mindful, but would act on our behalf.

I have been asked several times, "What's the point of the Bible?" From my perspective it's simple: The bottom line is that the Bible is all about relationship. A relationship God wants to have with each of us. Billy Graham would often sum up the Bible with a single verse, John 3:16 which says, *"For God so loved the world that He gave His one and only Son, that whoever believes in Him shall not perish but have eternal life."*

But, that raises the question: So What? So what if the Bible is the word from God. What possible difference does that make in my life today?

Well, for a Believer, it calls us to do our homework so we can discuss with a friend who is questioning and help them come to some answers. If we've not acted upon this Truth, the Bible is all about the relationship God wants to have with us, today. There's a reason for our beliefs, and we can hold to them without fear.

For some who are reading, you may be closer to becoming a Christian than you've ever imagined. Perhaps you have accepted the Bible, even understand the message and the purpose Jesus had for coming into the world. But you've never acted on that understanding. This is where we must move from head knowledge, to a heart decision.

The Bible tells us that God calls us to "reason" with Him (Isaiah 1:18). He has pursued us, He longs to care for us, and even when we weren't really interested in Him – He was still interested in us. And it hasn't changed since time began, as Ephesians 1:4 tells us, *"He chose us in him before the creation of the world."* The Bible tells us that knowing God shows us our purpose for living. In Acts 17:28 we read, *"In him we live and move and exist."* Knowing our Creator God will begin to unravel this mystery of why we are here. From one end of this incredible Book to the other, we discover a great truth. The truth is, God's plan has always been to give us life, a life worth living. And not what we often think, not just "pie in the sky when we die", but real life. Right here and right now. And the more we pursue, not only knowing about Him, but knowing Him – the more we will understand this gift of life He wants to give us.

When we come to know God, we know not only the Designer, but the Design for our life. Questions like, "Why am I here? How can I live a better life? How can I get rid of my past mistakes?", all begin to find a solution. Those solutions are found in God. The God of the universe is as close as a prayer and He waits to hear from us.

Chapter Three

A Unique Person

Around the world today there are billions of Christians who meet together on a regular basis. They meet together to pray, to worship and to celebrate Jesus' resurrection. They pray to Jesus, they ask forgiveness through Jesus, they worship Jesus, they call Him Savior and Lord. But why do Christians do that? What is the evidence that substantiates that He is worthy of that kind of attention? Upon what FACT can we base our belief in Him?

Four men recorded what Jesus said and did, we refer to their biographical work as the four Gospels – Matthew, Mark, Luke and John. As best as we can tell, Mark was the first of the Gospels. Now the argument has been made for years, that the Gospels were written some fifty to sixty years after the events. For that reason, most of the *facts* about Jesus, had been turned into *legends*. And the story about Jesus had become greatly exaggerated.

We have since learned that the Gospel of Mark was written as early as 35 or 36 A.D. The other Gospel accounts followed soon after. That would put the pen on the paper within 24 to 36 months of Jesus' life and ministry. Certainly well within a timeline to enable each writer to recall specific details to the events and teachings of Jesus.

John, one of His disciples, was present and heard first hand what Jesus taught. He records his account in what we call the Gospel of John. There was a purpose for John writing his account, as seen in John 20:30, where John writes, *"But these are written so that you may believe that Jesus is the Christ, the Son of God, and that by believing you may have life in his name."* As we look at each of the Gospel accounts, we can see that each have the same goal in mind, of introducing Jesus Christ to the world. Each Gospel was written with a different "reader" in mind. And ultimately, that people from all walks of life, from every corner of the earth would come to know Jesus and would accept Him as the Lord and Savior.

So what evidence is there to believe in this person called Jesus Christ? Why should anyone put their faith in this Man of Galilee? Even Thomas was offered evidence so that he would believe. And there are evidences upon which we can build a faith in the person of Jesus Christ. Three distinct pieces of evidence:

1. A Historical Person
Even the most ardent critic of Christianity will have to admit the existence of Jesus Christ is a historical fact. As documented by historians. The following is a short list of historians from the 1st Century who gave us historical record regarding the events of their day. Of those who are on this list, none are Christians, none were followers of Jesus Christ, all were simply historians used by the Romans to record the events of the day:

Flavius Josephus, the Jewish born-Roman hired historian from Jerusalem, records: *"there arose a great man, whom the leaders of his people had put to death by Pontius Pilate, and this person was called the Christ"*

Thallus another Roman historian from 50 A.D. writes: *"that at the time of the man named Christ crucifixion the sun failed to give light from noon until 3 o'clock"*

Tacitus, when writing about Nero's attempt to cover up his burning the city of Rome to the ground writes: *"Hence to suppress the rumor, he falsely charged with the guilt the persons commonly called Chrsitians. Christus the founder of the name was put to death by Pontius Pilate in the reign of Tiberius . . . "*

And the list goes on. More than a dozen historians from the first century tell us of the existence of Jesus of Nazareth. Some give only a quick reference to His existence. Many go on to tell us of His death by means of crucifixion during the reign of Pontius Pilate. So He was here, He walked upon this earth. When we talk about the person of Jesus Christ, we're talking about a real person, a person of history. Add to this a second piece of evidence.

2. A Person Of Prophecy

Long before Jesus actually walked on this earth, the Old Testament told us what to look for when the Messiah would arrive. Let's remember the Old Testament was in print 250 years before Christ was born. And for the criticism that says that the Bible has been changed over the years so that the prophecies match up with what Jesus did, remember the Dead Sea Scrolls. The Dead Sea Scrolls serve as a reminder that what we are reading today is the same as to what was being read 250 years before Jesus was born.

When we go to the Old Testament, we discover that there are over three hundred Prophecies regarding The Messiah. Of these three hundred prophecies there are, what is referred to, as the 60 Major Prophecies. These 60 major prophecies refer to such details as the fact that the Messiah

will be:	Born in Bethlehem	Micah 5:2
	Born Of A Virgin	Isaiah 7:14
	Appear in 2nd Temple	Hagai 2:7
	Sold for 30 Pieces	Zechariah 11:12
	Crucified With Sinners	Isaiah 53:12
	Hands & Feet Pierced	Psalms 22:16
	Side Pierced	Zechariah 12:10
	No Broken Bones	Psalms 34:20
	Gambled for Garment	Psalms 22:18
	Exact Time of Arrival	Daniel 9:25-26

Now Daniels prophecy is probably one of the most interesting. Daniel lived about 600 B.C. While in captivity under the Babylonians, he prophesied there would be a time line for when the Messiah would arrive. His prophecy found in Daniel 9:25 says, *"Know and understand this: From the issuing of the decree to restore and rebuild Jerusalem until the Anointed One, the ruler, comes, there will be seven 'sevens,' and sixty-two 'sevens.' It will be rebuilt with streets and a trench, but in times of trouble."* Daniel based his time line upon when the Israelites, who were slaves to the Babylonians, would be given permission to return to and rebuild the city of Jerusalem. That event, would measure when the Messiah would begin his public ministry. The exact time would be, *"seven sevens and sixty two sevens"* which equals, 483 years after the decree to restore Jerusalem.

Daniel's prophecy had to wait 150 years. And it would take a king by the name of Artaxerxes to make Daniel's prophecy come true. Artaxerxes, was a direct descendant of the Persian king Cyrus, who in 438 B.C. decreed the exiled Jews could return to Israel. It was Artaxerxes however who gave permission for the Jews to return to Jerusalem and rebuild the city, as best as we can tell, somewhere around 458 B.C.

Now remember, 483 years after the Jews were allowed to return, Daniel said the Messiah would appear. So let's do the math: 458 B.C. plus 483 years, puts us somewhere around 25 A.D. Keeping in mind that our present calendar may be off just a few years that puts, according to Daniel in 600 B.C., the Messiah beginning his public ministry somewhere between 25 – 29 A.D. According to all historical accounts, who shows up in 25–29 A.D. – Jesus of Nazareth! There is no other person of history who fulfills, not only Daniel's prophecy, not only the 60 Major Prophecies, but all 300 prophecies regarding the Messiah. But there's a third piece of evidence we need to look at.

3. Evidenced In Changed Lives Today

From the time Jesus walked the shores of Galilee, teaching the disciples, till today what Paul wrote still holds true: *"This same Good News (the Good News of Jesus Christ). . . is changing lives everywhere, just as it changed yours that very first day you heard and understood the truth about God's great kindness to sinners."* Col 1:6

What was true in the first century, is still true today. If only we could sit down with people, people from all over the world and listen to their life stories. Men and women of all ages, people from all walks of live, who have had their lives radically changed by power of Jesus Christ. Families that have been restored, marriages that have been put back together, lives that have been changed. All because people accepted His invitation, His offer to give them rest. And billions of people have found that promise to be true.

The criticism is that Christianity is for weak minded people. People who can't really think for themselves. But, the evidence speaks differently. Napoleon Bonaparte was an incredible military genius. He was exiled to an island to live out his life. While on that island, Napoleon had time to reflect on a lot of things, including the person of Jesus Christ. To which he concludes: *"Superficial minds see a resemblance between Christ and the founders of empires and other religions.That resemblance does not exist. There is between Christianity and every other religion in the world the distance of infinity."*

William Shakespeare in his will wrote: *"I commend my soul into the hands of God, hoping and assuredly believing, through the merits of Jesus Christ my Savior to be made partaker of life everlasting."*

Charles Dickens in his will wrote: *"I commit my soul to the mercy of God, through our Lord Jesus Christ. I now most solemnly impress upon you the truth and the beauty of the Christian faith."*

Leo Tolstoi after a life as an atheist said: *"For 35 years of my life I was a nihilist – not a revolutionary socialist, but a man who believed in nothing. Five years ago my faith came to me. I believed in the doctrine of Jesus and my whole life underwent a sudden transformation. Life and death ceased to be evil, instead of despair I tasted joy and happiness that death could not take away."*

Presidents, kings, teachers, doctors, lawyers, gifted people, intelligent men and women, people from all kinds of backgrounds and all intellectual levels, have come to the same conclusion: This person of history, this man of prophecy, this carpenter's son from Nazareth is a man who can be trusted. A Savior who can be trusted.

Just recently I had the opportunity to watch Christianity being challenged again. And from all places the Travel Channel. I watch the travel channel about three times a year. I look forward to seeing distant places and the scenery, and the boats. And this particular show took us to

India. A man was being interviewed who was going to show the viewers the "Tomb of Jesus". Unfortunately there was conflict in the area and he could not take us to the tomb. But, he knew where the tomb was and he described it to the host.

The hypothesis, that has been suggested many times over the years, is that Jesus didn't actually die on the cross. After he was taken down, he regained his strength and traveled to India.

Somewhere along the way the host asked the man: "How do you know it's the Tomb of Jesus?" Whereupon the man replied, "Everybody knows it's the tomb of Jesus. It's the only Christian tomb in a Hindu cemetery. The legend has it that's where Jesus was buried, so it must be him." Although I have several problems with this hypothesis my biggest is simply this:

After the crucifixion, Pontius Pilate sent a report to Tiberius Caesar in which he reports: *"And him (that is Christ) Herod, Archaelaus, Philip, Annas and Caiaphas, with all the people, delivered to me, making a great uproar against me that I should try him. I therefore ordered him to be crucified, having first scourged him, and having found against him no cause of evil accusations or deeds. And at the time he was crucified, there was darkness over all the world, the sun being darkened at mid-day, and the stars appearing, but in them there appeared no lustre; and the moon, as if turned into blood, failed in her light."*

You know what Pontius Pilate is saying? He is affirming what every other historical record from that time period is telling us: "I ordered his crucifixion, I supervised it, I was there when it happened. And he died on that cross." Please note in Pilate's report, that he had ordered the scourging (beating with whips) of Jesus.

The Roman historian, Josephus, tells us that Roman soldiers were proficient at scourging a person. He tells us that a well-trained Roman soldier could lay open the back of a prisoner, even to the point of exposing the spine, without killing the prisoner. Roman soldiers had the act of scourging down to an art, due in large part that they had plenty of opportunities to practice.

Scourging was administered by the use of a short whip made out of strips of leather. At the end of each strip of leather, was a piece of bone or metal and a stone or metal ball. The purpose of the metal ball, was to cause whelps (bruises) upon the body of the person being beaten. The whelps would fill with blood. Then when the pieces of stone or metal hit the whelps, more pain and more damage could be inflicted upon the person being beaten.

Now the Jews had a rule, regarding the beating of a person. When a convicted person was being beaten by an Israelite, they could not be beaten with more than forty lashes. So as a sign of mercy, no one was beaten with more than thirty-nine lashes, just in case someone had miscounted during the ordeal. The Romans had no such rule. Their only rule was simple, a person being beaten by a Roman soldier, was beaten until the Roman soldiers got tired of beating them. And Roman beatings could take hours.

Do you think the Romans soldiers took it easy on Jesus? Do you think there was any restraint or mercy shown? No way. Jesus was just like all the rest who had been tortured and beaten by Roman soldiers. There was no leniency, no mercy due to the "possibility" that Jesus just might be the King of the Jews. In fact all the more reason for the Roman soldiers to show the power of the Roman Empire. The power to crush anyone, including the King of the Jews, who dared to go against them.

Then after beating Jesus with no mercy, with no limits, they paraded Him through town. And though it may sound cruel to us, the parade was actually an act of mercy on the part of the Romans. The purpose of the parade was first of all, an opportunity for all the inhabitants of the city to identify the person who was going to be crucified. Then if there was anyone who had evidence to prove that the prisoner should not be crucified, to bring such evidence to the attention of the Roman authorities and the prisoner would be set free.

The second purpose, was much less merciful. It was a demonstration of Rome's power. Another opportunity for everyone witnessing the demonstration to get a very clear message, "This is what happens to anyone who messes with the Roman Empire."

The parade would end at a point of geographical significance: a road leading into town, a busy intersection, a hill that could be seen at a distance. Again the Romans had one thing in mind, a show of strength. Anyone traveling in or out of town, any walking through the streets and looking up at the hill, could see Rome's power on display. And in Jesus' situation, He was taken to a hill just outside the city gates. A place called Golgotha. Golgotha was a place where crucifixions were administered on a regular basis.

Crucifixion was a common means of punishing and executing prisoners by the Romans. The pictures we have hanging in churches and in portraits, of a finished, well sanded, evenly-balanced cross are misleading. Crosses were made out of whatever materials were available. And Roman soldiers were again, extremely proficient in cross building and crucifixions. They had plenty of practice.

The soldiers took whatever lumber that could be found that would accomplish their purpose, and would then nail two or three pieces together. Sometimes, in the form of a T, sometimes in the form of an X. Whatever would support the weight of their prisoner. Laying the lumber on the ground, they would stretch out the arms of their prisoner, placing a long metal spike just above the wrist, taking a wooden mallet they would literally nail the person to the cross. Then the soldiers would take the feet and crossing them, they would again drive the spike through the feet, pinning the person to the cross. Whereupon, the cross would be lifted up and dropped into a hole in the ground, suspending the person for all to see. The weight of the person was held in place by the spikes.

The one being executed, would then be left to die. Most often death came from exposure. But on many occasions, when the crucifixion was more "public", or when it served Rome's purposes, a more systematic process was used.

The Romans would leave the person on the cross, the weight of their own body pulling on the metal spikes. As the weight of their body became heavier and heavier; it would begin to pull down on their arms, constricting the muscles in the upper chest, making it more and more difficult for the person to breathe. So they would lift themselves by using their legs, an extremely painful process as they pushed against the pins holding their feet in place. When they could no longer stand the pain, they would relax, causing the body to once again constrict breathing and the process would start over. Again and again, lifting and relaxing, until eventually the person had no strength left and they would die of asphyxiation.

This form of execution would normally take several hours to accomplish. The Romans would allow crowds to gather, to witness the event. But after a few hours the crowds would disperse and the Romans would then expedite the death by a very simple process of one of two means. The first being a Roman soldier would take a heavy object, a mallet or a large stone, and break the legs of the victim, thus making it impossible for the person to lift themselves any more. Death by asphyxiation would occur in just a few minutes.

The second would be in the form of a Roman soldier taking a spear and driving the spear through the rib cage of the person, puncturing the lungs and most often the heart. In Jesus' case, this is exactly what the soldier did. The Bible records that *blood and water* came flowing from the wound, an indication that fluid had collected around the heart and that Jesus was dead already.

Here's a question we need to ask, do you think the Roman guard ever stopped and thought "You know there's an Old Testament prophecy that said that his bones would not be broken, but his side would be pierced. Maybe I should do something in order to fulfill that Old Testament prophecy?" No way. The last thought any of those Roman guards had on their minds, was fulfilling some Old Testament prophecy. When the Romans came to Jesus, they discovered He had already died and to assure that He was in fact dead, they did what they had done a hundred if not thousands of executions before, they ran a spear up through His side to make sure He was dead.

Here's the point: the problem with Jesus or anyone else, surviving a Roman cross and traveling to India or England or North Dakota is beyond reason. If a person reached the point where the Romans decided it was time to be crucified, if a person went to the cross, they did not come down alive. The purpose of the cross was not only execution, but a demonstration of Rome's power. And a clear message, "Don't mess with the Roman Empire." For anyone to come down alive, would be an embarrassment to the Roman Empire. And Jesus was no exception.

But even well trained Roman soldiers can have, well, problems. Something went wrong after the crucifixion. They put Him in a grave, just as they were supposed to do. They rolled a stone across the entrance, just as they were supposed to do. They stationed a squad of soldiers to guard the tomb, just as they were supposed to do. But it didn't work! They buried Him on Friday, when they came back on Sunday, He was gone! Just as He had promised.

So this raises a very good question, "So What? So what if Jesus is who He claims to be? What does that mean to me?" It means this; if Jesus fulfilled all the prophecies, if He was in fact nailed to a cross as a sacrifice for us, if He did raise from the dead, then He is everything He claims to be. And if He is everything He claims to be, then He Can Keep His Word! He can forgive our wrongs, He can show us a life that is truly worth living, and when Jesus says, *"Come to me, all you who weary and heavy laden, and I will give you rest."* He can and does do that for anyone willing to trust Him. When Jesus said: *"Don't let your hearts be troubled. Trust in God, and trust in me. I am going to prepare a place for you. After I go and prepare a place for you, I will come back and take you to be with me so that you may be where I am"*, those were not just empty words on a page. He is able to keep His promises. And we can take Him up on His offer to enable us to live a life that's worth the living. He can, and will do everything He has promised!

Over the past 2000 years, people from all kinds of backgrounds, from all kinds of cultures, from all walks of life have taken up His offer to *"cast all our cares on Him"*. That is not a hopeless effort. There are reasons why people have believed in Him. And though not everyone has used the identical same evidence to come to a conclusion, every Believer has had to base their choice to follow Him on some evidence. And that evidence is available to anyone who would be willing to investigate for themselves whether His claims are true. It's an investigation that could bring incredible changes in our lives.

Chapter Four

Only One Way?

Christians believe in the person of Jesus, who He is and the claims He made. Jesus made a variety of claims during His ministry. Besides being able to forgive sin, Jesus also claimed that He is the only way to God. In John 14:6, Jesus said, *"I am the way, and the truth and the life. No one comes to the Father but by Me."* Now for a lot of people that sounds narrow-minded, even snobbish. Even in a country that has a strong belief in Jesus. In a 2004 Newsweek Poll of 1,009 U.S. adults conducted by Princeton Survey Research Association, found 82% of those surveyed believed that Jesus was God or the Son of God.

So why, in a country that has such a strong believe in the Deity of Jesus, is His statement so controversial? With this single statement, Jesus touches on a number of America's *nerves.* Things we believe in this country, but things that are challenged by Jesus' claim. Let's look at some of the leading beliefs in our country. We often believe:

1. All Religions Are The Same
A growing number of Americans are convinced that when you get right down to it, when you strip away all different distinctions of the wide-variety of religions in America, all religions basically teach the same thing. So it doesn't really matter which one a person believes. As you may have heard someone say, "All spiritual paths, lead up the same

mountain to God." Which is another way of saying, "It doesn't matter what you believe, just so long as you believe something." Yet with this one incredibly outlandish claim, Jesus Christ boldly places Christianity in a class all by itself. If Jesus claim is true, that He is the only path to God, then the reality is this: Christianity cannot be reconciled with any other religion. In Acts 4:12 we read, *"Salvation is found in no one else for there is no other name under heaven given to men by which we must be saved."* The uniqueness of Christianity is founded in the uniqueness of Jesus Christ. He is unlike any other religious leader who ever walked on this planet. The difference between other religious leaders and Jesus is based first of all in what they taught.

While other religious leaders taught, "I'll show you how to find many truths." Jesus taught, *"I am the truth."* While other religious leaders taught, "I'll show you many ways to salvation." Jesus taught, *"I am the way to eternal life."* While other religious leaders taught, "I'll show you many ways to God." Jesus taught, *"I am the way."* There is a big difference between these teachings. For the longest time we Americans have tried to find commonality between the different religions of the world. But there are major differences between Christianity and all other belief systems.

Americans often view the various religions, Christianity included, as humankinds effort to reach out to God. But Christians believe that Jesus Christ is God's attempt to reach out to humankind. And that this was demonstrated by what Jesus did and what He taught.

When we sit down and take a good look at what Jesus taught, His teachings strike a chord within us. For example Jesus taught that we are all guilty of wrongdoing. And if we take a good look at ourselves, we know that's true. None of us can claim to be perfect. That truth resonates with our life experience. Then Jesus went on to teach, that our wrongdoing has separated us from God. And again, we know from our experience that is true, as well.

Ask yourself for a minute, has there ever been a time in your life when you've felt that God was distant, detached from you? Of course. We've all felt that. Why? Because our wrongdoings created a separation between us and God. We sense the purity of God and recognize that we don't measure up to that standard.

Now because God, by His nature, is a righteous judge, our wrongdoing must be paid for. And out of His love for us, Jesus Christ volunteered to be our substitute, to pay the penalty for the sin that we deserve, so that we wouldn't have to. Jesus, in essence, became the bridge by which we can come back to a relationship with God.

Christians believe there is a huge difference between *good works* and *grace*. All other religions focus on the things we must do, some sort of religious ritual, some sort of way to pay for our wrongs, some way to try to please God. The problem is we don't know how many good things we have to do in order to please God. Perhaps you've heard someone say, "If I have enough good things to balance out the bad things in my life, I can get to heaven." But when is good enough, good enough? I don't know about you, but I can't keep up on the list of mistakes I have made in my lifetime.

Christianity, on the other hand, says you can never do enough *good* to earn your way into heaven. Jesus has done what we could never do. By His sacrifice on the cross, it has been done for us. He lived the perfect sinless life and He went to the cross to pay for the sins of the world. And while on the cross He underscored this reality when He said, *"It is finished."* Everything that needed to be done to build the bridge back to God was accomplished by His death. And all that's left for us is to apply that to our life, to receive His free gift of forgiveness and grace and mercy.

2. All Truths Are Equal
In other words, let's say Christianity is unique, different than every other religion in the world. It's still just one philosophy among many. It's only as valid as any other religious systems. Even if there are some differences they all have equal claims on the truth. Have you ever heard someone say, "You have your truth and I have mine." They're both equally true.

This sits well with us as Americans because we live in a tolerant society. Our founding Fathers came to this country so that there could be freedom *of* religion. The Bill of Rights and our Constitution protects the right of any human being to believe whatever they want to believe. And because of that respect of different beliefs, we make the erroneous assumption that because the laws of our country protect every belief, every belief must be equally true. And that's not the case.

From our very beginning as a nation, our Founding Fathers sought to have a country with the freedom to exchange ideas, even if those ideas are wrong. In other words, truth and falsehood could be expressed openly and each person could determine for themselves which was the truth. They were convinced that in the end, truth would prevail.

In our country we have seen many beliefs exchanged. People have believed in the God of the Bible and people have believed in the god of Haley's Comet. Even in the name of Christianity extreme teachings have been perpetuated. For example, in 1998 Rulon Jeffs, the father of Warren Jeffs, proclaimed that the end of the world was near and that God told him that He wanted the congregation, to move to Hillsdale Utah or Colorado City Arizona. Rulon Jeffs died in 2002, the end of the world not happening during his lifetime as he "prophesied".

In this country we have seen the Rulon Jeffs', the Jim Jone's and the David Koresh's. Our Constitution protecting their rights to believe whatever they chose. But that protection in no way implies that what they believed and what they taught others to believe is The Truth. Just because all religions are equally protected does not mean that all religions are equally true. Each person in this country must evaluate the truth and weigh the evidence to determine which Belief is reliable to base their life and their future upon.

So how can we know that the claims that Jesus made are trustworthy? As we have been doing in this book, we must look at the evidence:

A. Jesus validates His claim to being the only way to God by His fulfilling the many prophecies that were written hundreds of years before He was even born. Nobody has been able to do this except Jesus Christ. A thorough investigation of the prophecies made about the Messiah reveals they were not prophecies He could manipulate. He couldn't have arranged for His place of birth, His ancestry, the manner of His death and more.

B. Jesus validates His claim by His character. We have seen many times in this country that public leaders often disguise who they truly are. They play well to the crowd, but in their private lives, they turn out to be very disappointing. But the opposite was true of Jesus. As His followers spent time with Him, getting to know Him more, they increasingly marveled at His purity, His holiness and His integrity. Nobody was closer to Jesus than Peter and John and after spending three years of being with Him day after day, John's assessment of Jesus was, *"In Him is no sin."* Peter's observation was similar, *"He committed no sin and no deceit was found in His mouth."*

Jesus' character stands the test of His claim to being the only way to God.

C. Jesus validated His claim by what He did. Jesus challenged anyone who would ever believe in Him in John 10:37, *"Don't believe in Me unless I do miracles of God."* In other words, anyone can claim to be the Son of God but unless they can handle the supernatural as evidence, don't believe them and don't even believe Me. When we look at the historic record, Jesus did some pretty incredible things. And they weren't done in some remote place, in some quiet corner, with just a couple of people watching. The miracles He performed were in broad daylight, in front of skeptics and believers. Open to anyone's investigation as to their validity. So His ability to do the miraculous further validates His claims of who He was.

D. His most spectacular demonstration was fulfilling His own prediction that three days after He was put to death He would rise from the dead. This was witnessed by more than 500 eyewitnesses, not just the 12 Disciples. People talked with Him, walked with Him, ate a meal with Him and were even invited to reach out and touch Him. Who else but the Son of God could spend three days in a tomb and then come forward and establish that He had in fact returned to life? Christianity is not just another philosophy, it is a reality. Jesus didn't just claim that He's the one and only way to God, He validated His claims and fully established His credibility. But there's a third claim we need to consider:

3. Christianity Is Exclusive

The idea that believing only in Jesus, excludes anyone else from ever entering Heaven. The reality is that Jesus' offer is extremely "inclusive". In John 3:16 Jesus says, *"For God so loved the world that He gave His only Son, that whosoever believes in Him would have eternal life."* The reality is we all have a terminal disease, a disease called sin. The reason Christians cling to Jesus is because He is the perfect physician. He's the only one who has the cure for our disease. We can try to pay for our sins by doing good deeds but it hasn't worked. We can ignore our problem and hope it just goes away but it hasn't. We can sincerely believe there are other ways of dealing with our sin but we would be sincerely wrong. The truth is, only the Perfect Physician offers the cure for the disease of our sin. And His offer is open to any and all when He said, *"Come unto Me, you who are weary and heavy laden, and I will give you rest."* And when any of us turn to Jesus Christ, we are acting based on evidence.

Now it's true (and sad) that sometimes Christians act in a way that is contrary to their reality. They conduct themselves that somehow they may be a little better than someone else. But reality is difference. The reality is, at the foot of the Cross we are all standing on level ground. He doesn't care about our economic level, or our ethnic background, or what title we may or may not have, or what mistakes we have made in the past. His offer is for anyone who is willing. He will give not only forgiveness of sin, but life that is worth living, now and forever.

Someone once said, "A Christian is just one beggar telling another beggar where to find food." And that's a pretty good description. The history of Christianity has been marred by the misconduct of so called "believers" who detoured from the life Christ intended for His people. A life focused on caring for others in this world who had a need. Just as He cared for any who had a need, even if they chose never to follow Him, even if they called for His crucifixion. This life should be based on humility and respect for others. Too often Christians miss that mark. And even then we realize how much we need God, how much we need a Savior, to work in our lives to enable us to become more than just people taking up time and space on this Pale Blue Dot.

Chapter Five

A Quiet Conversation

Christians pray. Well, it's not just Christians. In a 2007 survey, more than four out of five Americans (83%) had prayed in the last week. Now while all Americans are not praying to the same God, it is a resounding insight to the spiritual tone of our country. Every day of the week, Americans are praying. We're asking God for help, for insight, for forgiveness, for strength, and for hope.

Recent medical studies reveal that praying has a strong and healthy affect on the human body. Prayer calms the nerves, lowers blood pressure, relaxes tight muscles, produces more serotonin in the brain and generally is good for the overall health of the one praying. And even for those who are being prayed for. In a study conducted by Dr. Targ in 1995 to 1996 amongst AIDs patients in a San Francisco hospital, researchers discovered there was improved disease progression, a decrease in medical utilization and improved psychological well-being amongst the patients who were being prayed for. But there is more to prayer for Christians that the health benefits.

Step into any assembly of Christians on a Sunday morning and we'll hear; the Prayer of the Rosary, the Sinner's Prayer, the Lord's Prayer or a variety of recited prayers. But watch the people as they pray those prayers; eyes often closed, head sometimes bowed, hands perhaps raised, all in quiet reverence. Because Christians pray, expectantly. Yes, their motives are often self serving; we want God to solve a problem, heal a disease, show us a sign, or open the door to employment. But the reality is Christians pray because they are reliant upon, hopeful in and expectant of God to work in their lives. The motives are not always self serving. There is a reason for this expectancy.

More than fifty times throughout the Gospels accounts Jesus teaches Believers to ask, pray, receive and expect God to work in their lives. His most direct instructions are found in Matthew chapter seven, a part of what we call the Sermon On The Mount, where He teaches, *"Ask and it will be given to you; seek and you will find; knock and the door will be opened to you. For everyone who asks receives; he who seeks finds; and to him who knocks, the door will be opened. "Which of you, if his son asks for bread, will give him a stone? Or if he asks for a fish, will give him a snake? If you, then, though you are evil, know how to give good gifts to your children, how much more will your Father in heaven give good gifts to those who ask him! So in everything, do to others what you would have them do to you, for this sums up the Law and the Prophets."* In these few words and in other teachings of Christ, Christians base their trust in prayer.

But Jesus goes on to teach that prayer is not limited to the benefit of the one praying. He teaches Believers to, *"You have heard it said, Love your neighbor and hate your enemies. But I tell you: Love your enemies and pray for those who persecute you"* And across America and around the world Christians pray for those who oppose Christianity on every hand. And in that dichotomy we discover the real reason why Christians pray, because Jesus told us to.

But this raises a good question, "If we pray, does God answer?" Jesus replies to that question in John 14:14, *"You may ask me for anything in my name, and I will do it."* Later in the New Testament James writes, *"You have not, because you do not ask God. When you ask, you do not receive, because you ask with wrong motives, that you may spend what you get on your pleasures."* There is no question God is willing to respond to our prayers, the greater question is, "Why don't I hear from God?" If there is any "secret" in the Christian life, that secret would be, how do we hear from God? There are four important steps we must pursue in order to hear from God.

1. Develop An Open Heart

In order to hear God speak, we must first want to hear Him speak. We must desire it, be teachable about it, be receptive to it, eager and ready to learn. We must develop an open mind and an open heart to God. Many times we don't hear God speak because we've already made up our minds what we want to do, or what we want to hear. We don't even consider there could be other possibilities. Possibilities that we have not thought of, possibilities only God is aware of. We've closed our minds and hardened our heart, so God never gets through.

In the Parable of the Sower Jesus warns against developing a hardened heart. This is the person with a closed mind. The person who says they want to hear from God, but their heart and their mind is already closed to the possibility. What causes any of us to be so defensive? Why is it that sometimes we don't really want to hear God speak? There are three possible answers:

A. Fear makes us suspicious of God. We're afraid of what He might say. He might alter our lifestyle or make some change in us. We may have to make some restitution for something we've done or even seek forgiveness from someone we've wronged. We might have to do something we really don't want to do. But the reality is God loves us and has our best interest at heart. Jesus explained it thusly, *"Which of you, if his son asks for bread, will give him a stone? Or if he asks for a fish, will give him a snake? If you, then, though you are evil, know how to give good gifts to your children, how much more will your Father in heaven give good gifts to those who ask him!"* The changes God wants to make in our lives are always for our best.

B. Pride causes us to be defiant toward God. We convince ourselves into thinking we don't need God's advise. We can make it on our own. We know whats best for us and God doesn't really understand our situation, so we are the best judge of what is right for us. Pride, more often than not, is just a smoke screen for our insecurity. We are so afraid of our weaknesses, we don't want to admit them, even to ourselves. So our pride becomes a barrier to hearing God.

C. Bitterness because of our life experiences may cause us to be defensive toward God. It is a truth about life, we all get hurt at times. And sometimes our response to that hurt is to build a wall so nobody can get close. We build a wall so even God can't get through. Our bitterness can make us cynical, callous, and hardened. We remained fixed on the question,"Why did God let that happen?" In the process we become defensive. The tragedy of a bitter life is that it bears no fruit. Nothing can grow in the wasteland of our heart. So it's no wonder that James prompts us to, *"Get rid of all moral filth and the evil that is so prevalent, and humbly accept the Word planted in you, which can save you."* We have to tear down the barriers and develop an open heart to hear from God. Which leads us to the next step:

2. Find Time To Listen And Minimize Distractions
In the rush our of times, we don't slow down for much. We are bombarded on a daily basis with sound and images. Let's face it, most of us can't even take a walk around the block without our Ipod! So we become accustomed to the noise. And with the constant demand of our attention from advertisments, TV programs, the latest gadget we need to buy,very little of our attention span is left for things that matter most. Like hearing from God.

Have you ever wondered why God chose Mary to be the mother of Jesus? The simple answer is, when God spoke, Mary listened. The Bible records, *"Mary pondered these things in her heart."* Mary was thoughtful. When God spoke, she didn't just let it run in one ear and out the other, she thought about it, she pondered it. All too often we are in such a hurry, our prayer is more like, "Speak, God, but do it quick! I've only got this commercial before my shows back on!" We've got to allocate time if we want to hear God speak. In the Parable of the Sower Jesus uses the illustration of seed as a metaphor for hearing from God, *"Other seed fell on shallow soil with rock beneath. This seed began to grow but soon it withered and died for lack of moisture . . . Those on the rock are the ones who receive the Word with joy when they heard it, but they have no root. They believe for a while, but in the time of testing, they fall away."*

Jesus says the shallow soil represents a superficial heart, a busy life. This is the impulsive person who reacts emotionally to the moment, but fails to take the time to build a life on hearing from God. If we want to hear God speak, we have to cultivate an open heart and set aside the time to really hear what He has to say.

Jesus was explaining why we have such a tough time hearing from God, *"Other seed fell among thorns which grew up with it and choked the plants . . . The seed that fell among thorns stands for those who hear, but as they go on their way, they are choked by life's worries, riches, and pleasures, and they don't mature."* The soil with weeds represents a preoccupied heart, a busy schedule, a full day. We're just too busy to hear God. We've got so many things going on in our minds, we just can't hear God.

Someone once said, "Beware of the barrenness of a busy life." We can be so busy making a living, we fail to make a life. Jesus warns us to be aware that in our fast paced world there are many demands on our time. There are so many voices vieing for our attention, clamoring for our focus. As a result we become diluted, not really committed to anything, especially taking the time to hear from God. To hear from God we need to make the time to listen, and eliminate the distractions. And finally we need to:

3. Be Ready To Cooperate With God

Jesus was trying to help His Disciples understand why it was difficult for some to follow Him, *"He who has ears, let him hear."* God speaks to those who have chosen in advance to be responsive to His voice. To follow God's lead, to do what God instructs. God is not willing to say, "I'll tell you what I want you to do, then you can decide whether you want to do it or not." No. We need to decide in advance we are willing to do whatever He tells us to do, then He opens up windows of Heaven. Again Jesus uses a Parable to teach us, *"The seed on good soil stands for those with a noble and good heart, who hear the word, retain it and by persevering produces a crop."* The good soil represents a responsive heart, the heart that says, "Lord, I'm willing in advance, to do whatever you want me to do." When we take that attitude, then we are tuned in to God. Remember: *"He who seeks shall find. He who knocks the door shall be opened."* God is anxious to speak with us! When are willing to eliminate the distractions, set aside the time, cooperate with Him in advance.

That brings us to the result of prayer. The result is a life of purpose and direction. A life that is productive and worth the living. God wants to give our lives depth. Because life does bring disappointments and struggles. But prayer is a fortress of strength. Christians pray because they are convinced God not only hears, but is willing and able to move in the lives of any and all who call to Him. And though we may pray with our agenda in mind, Christians have a confidence that God has and will show a better way to live.

Chapter Six

The Inner Struggle

It may seem strange that we should address the issue of doubt. Because with all we might say, with all the evidence we might look at on why to believe in God, or the Bible, or the person of Jesus, the fact remains that sometimes we doubt. Jesus understood this as He addressed this issue with his Disciples just hours before His crucifixion. In John 14:1 Jesus said, *"Let not your hearts be troubled, trust in God, trust also in Me."*

We need to deal with this issue because somewhere along the way, we all wrestle with doubt. Several times a year someone will call me, or stop by my office and say, "I need some help. I've got more questions than answers. There are times I've wondered whether I'm a Christian at all. I don't think God hears my prayers. I don't think God even exists. I don't think I belong here, or any church." As awkward as these conversations are, I love to have these kinds of talks. Know why? Because those are times when we're not playing church. We're not afraid to speak the truth, to say out loud, "I've got some serious doubts about God."

Has that ever crossed your mind? Has the question ever come to your mind "What if this Christianity thing isn't true at all? What if, when you die, you just die? Maybe there's nothing to be done about all the wrongs I have done in my life? Can the Bible can really be trusted by a rational thinking person in the 21st century?" And try as we may to have "confidence" we still have a lot of questions.

Before we go any further, we need to recognize that doubt is not a terrible thing. In fact, for anyone who has seriously considered the claims of Jesus Christ, or has seriously considered what it means to be a Christian, there's going to be a time when questions, even some doubts come up over one thing or another. That's not limited to Christians. It is a common experience among people who "think through" their convictions about faith or any other important issue. And just having doubt reveals the issue is important enough to give serious thought to.

So it's not whether or not we're ever going to have doubts. The issue is what do you do, once you have doubt? How do you keep doubt from destroying your faith? It's important we explore the issue of doubt.

Have you ever thought about what doubt is? There's a lot of misconceptions about doubt. For some people doubt is the opposite of faith. But it's not. Actually the opposite of faith is unbelief. And there's a big difference between unbelief and doubt. What is unbelief? Unbelief is a willful refusal to believe. It's a deliberate choice to deny God. But that's not doubt.

Doubt is to be indecisive over an issue. It's being caught between the certain and the uncertain. Between the definite and the indefinite. It's knowing the facts, but wrestling with the reality. We may have legitimate questions about some facet of the Christian faith and still be a Believer. We can be a fully-committed, sold-out follower of Jesus Christ and still have some doubts.

Now the question may come to mind, "If there is so much evidence for why we should believe in God, in the Bible, in the person of Christ, why would anyone have doubts? If the evidence is so overwhelming, why would anyone ever have doubts?" The reality is that most of us have doubts about a lot of believes we hold to. Let's take a look at a couple of causes for doubt, there are more than the few we are looking at, but these will be enough to get us started. Some of the causes for doubt are:

1. We Think A Lot About Things

For some of us, we are deep contemplative thinkers. We are forever "going over" things in our mind. This continual process of questioning, analyzing, working it over in our minds, brings an endless number of questions. It's possible, if we are always asking questions, we may never get around to giving any answers.

Do you know anyone who always plays, "Devil's advocate"? They are forever asking the questions, but never getting to any answers. Part of the reason for this is because it's a lot easier to ask questions than to find answers. To sit outside a situation and hurl in a few choice questions seems so, academic. But it may never lead to finding any answers.

Several years ago, I was asked to speak at a church on a series of topics. Following each of the sessions, there were two people who would come to me with a list of "mistakes" I had made during my presentation. (Trust me, on any given occasion this can be a lengthy list.) Along with their list of mistakes, they had a series of "questions" for me. As we spoke, it became apparent, they weren't looking for answers. They just wanted to ask the questions. Now asking questions, is not a bad thing. In no way do I want to minimize the importance of thinking about or asking about the things of God. But we need to be as interested in finding the answers as we are in asking the questions.

2. Our Own Personal Struggles

Sometimes we doubt, because of sin in which we continue to participate. As we struggle with what we know is wrong, it causes us to continually question whether God has truly forgiven us, whether Jesus really did pay the penalty for our sin, whether we are "worthy" to be in God's family.

There is a price tag to sin in our lives. Sin creates a distance between us and God. Now God did not move from us, we moved from Him because of defiance. And with this distance comes feelings like "Where's God? Why don't I feel His presence in my life?" And we begin to doubt that He's there at all.

In times like this, we must realize that our doubts are not based on a lack of evidence, or God not keeping His word. Our doubts are based upon what's going on inside of us.

And it's not until we come to terms with what has separated us from God, that we will be able to address the doubt we are struggling with.

But it's also true that our doubts often come because of how we "feel" about God, or faith. Faith is not about feelings and emotions. Faith is a decision of the will to follow Jesus Christ. It's a choice that we make. Our faith isn't based on how emotionally charged up we are. When doubt comes because of not "feeling" right, we need to question the feelings rather than questioning our faith.

3. When We Face Disappointing Circumstances

Another reason for our doubt can be, simply put, disappointment with God. Perhaps we needed God to do something in our lives in a miraculous way. Perhaps we were in a crisis and God should have done - but He didn't. And in those circumstances, those expectations that were not met, became the reason for our doubting. And the truth is even Christians who mean well can contribute to this confusion.

Several years ago a family in the church where I was pastor, had their three year old daughter fall into a pool and drown. It was an accident of the worse kind. Someone had left a gate open, the little girl slipped away from her parents just long enough for a tragedy to happen. Unless we have lost a child, we can't imagine the agony those parents wrestled with as they waited at the hospital.

While these grief stricken parents are waiting at the hospital, a well meaning, but insensitive member of the church, met them in the waiting room to tell them that this was all part of "God's plan". Can you imagine what was going through their minds at that moment? Waiting for the doctor to give them word whether their child is even alive, and then to be told, "This is all part of God's plan." There's no question to why they would think, "If God is so cruel to take our daughter this way, we don't want anything to do with Him."

For about a week after the loss of their daughter this family had people calling, stopping by the house, bringing food. Then the calls stopped, the visits became fewer and all their friends got back to a "normal" life. Except, this family had no "normal" life to return too. There was emptiness in their house and in their hearts. And that emptiness brought up serious questions about God.

But we had this Elder at the church. You know those guys who can't do anything right? Every day, after work, this Elder, would go to this families home and sit. They would sit on the front porch, sit around the kitchen table. Sometimes they would talk, sometimes they would cry, on many a day, there was absolute silence. But for months he did one thing – he listened. He wasn't there to defend God. He wasn't there to somehow explain why God allowed something like this to happen to their family. He had one objective, he was there to simply care for this family.

After a few months, this Elder and these heart broken parents began to talk. The conversations were not comfortable, there were no "quick & easy answers" these parents would settle for. And this Elder was wise enough not to try and give those answers. Eventually, after several months, the parents began attending another church and became active in ministry again. In large part, because one single Elder, had taken the time to help them process their doubts and come to their own conclusions.

I learned a valuable lesson through that situation. Sometimes we Christians are way too quick to give answers. Answers to questions people aren't even asking. I know what it's like to be in a situation where you "ought" to say something. There ought to be some words to defend or explain why God has allowed something to happen. And for many believers, situations like this are seen as evangelistic opportunities. The question I ask myself, and I am convinced every Christian should ask: "How did Jesus handle situations like this?" And if we look, we'll discover He always showed incredible grace and mercy. His first priority was caring for people.

Many of us have gone through circumstances where we expected God to do, but He didn't. And it often takes time to move from questioning, to trusting.

4. Our Misguided Allegiance

Several years ago a young lady came to me with a problem. Her problem was, "I have this really cool professor at the college I'm attending. He spends time with his students. Instead of running off to the teachers lounge at lunch, he eats lunch with the students. He comes to all the activities. He's genuinely interested in us. And we all like him. He's very open and helps us with just about anything. Except when it comes to church, or God, or Christianity. Then he becomes very upset. He says religion is for the "weak minded". He makes a lot of sense and I don't always know how to handle his reasons why anyone is wasting their time in a church."

There are times when doubt is brought on by the people we look up to. It may be a coach, a teacher, a good friend, or a mentor, people we respect, who don't really understand the influence they have on other people. And if this person we truly admire, has some serious questions about God and faith, well maybe we should reconsider what we believe as well.

It is difficult to separate our respect of a person, from the fact they are not 100% right about everything. We need to remember, we can still admire the person, respect and listen to what they have to say, while realizing we may have something to share with them as well. After all, they are just like us, maybe older, maybe wiser, but they are still "just people". And people can be mistaken about a lot of things.

But this does raise the issue, how can we share a deep conviction we have about something, without dishonoring the people we respect? There is a way to accomplish that intention. If we are truly attempting to reason with people we care about, if we are seeking to openly discuss an issue that truly is important to us, there are four questions we need to ask:

1. Have you ever considered the possibility that you could be wrong about this issue?
2. If you were wrong, would you want to know?
3. If you discovered you had made a mistake, would you be willing to do something about it?
4. Could I share with you the evidence upon which why I have come to this conclusion?

It is possible for us to disagree with people we respect and still hold them in high estimation, to disagree without being disagreeable. Just because they are people we look up to, does not make them perfect. We should be evaluating and investigating any input we receive regarding things that are important, such as faith

It's been said that wrestling with the issues of life does not show a lack of faith, nor a lack of trust in God. In fact that's what faith is all about. But somewhere along the way we got this notion that if we doubt, then we are less a Christian, or we're not as good a Christian as someone who doesn't doubt.

Have you ever noticed the people in the Bible who served God, but had doubts? From one end of the Book to the other, you will find people just like us. People who served God faithfully, not perfectly, but faithfully and still had doubts. People like Moses, Abraham, Joseph, Elijah, Elisha, King David, Ezra, Peter, Thomas, even Paul. People who did incredible things for God, but were not without their own doubts at times. But, those doubts did not stop them.

As much as we worry about our doubts, doubts can sometimes be a helpful stimuli to our faith. Coming to terms with questions we have, can give us a hardier, more enduring, more resilient faith. There needs to be times when good battles with evil, when faith gets questioned by life experiences. Without those testing grounds, how can our faith stand on its own power?

That's the kind of faith many of us are after: a faith that has looked doubt straight in the eye and made it blink. God never intended for any of us to have the kind of faith that shrinks back from the tough issues, or is afraid to get on the firing line of real life. As we come to terms with our questions, with our doubts, our faith is only going to be made stronger having been tested by doubt.

So this raises the question, "How do I use my doubts to move me to a greater faith? How can I turn my doubts into faith?" I don't want to suggest this is an easy thing. Nor is it something that happens over night. There is a journey each of us must take in order to have a faith refined by the fires of doubt. There are, however, some Biblical principles that we can follow that can strengthen our faith.

1. Don't Minimize Our Doubt

On one occasion Jesus was trying to teach his disciples about overcoming their doubts. You may recall the occasion when Jesus invited Peter to step out of the boat and walk on the water. Half way to Jesus, Peter began to sink. The narrative tells us that Peter had taken more notice of the wind and waves, than he had of Jesus. His mistake was taking his eyes off of Jesus. It was then we read in Matthew 14:31, *"Jesus immediately reached out his hand and caught him, saying to him, You of little faith, why did you doubt?"*

Notice Jesus doesn't minimize Peter's doubt, but neither does He exaggerate his doubt. Without stepping out of the boat, Peter would never have had the opportunity for his faith to be tested, to be made stronger. And remember, Peter did walk on the water. Not very far, but a lot farther than I ever have.

Do you remember John the Baptist? The guy with the camel-skin coat, in the wilderness, eating honey and locusts? In the estimation of many, one of the most outstanding people found in the Bible. If there was ever anyone who should have been absolutely convinced who Jesus is, it would have been John the Baptist. Look at what John said regarding Jesus. It was John who pointed at Jesus and said, *"Behold the Lamb of God who takes away the sin of the world."* It was John who baptized Jesus in the Jordon river and saw the heavens open and heard the voice of God say, *"This is My Son in whom I am well pleased."*

It was John who directed the attention of the crowd to Jesus and then said, *"I have seen and I testify that this is the Son of God."*

Here's a person of incredible faith. But then what happens? He gets arrested. He gets thrown in prison. He gets word that he's going to be beheaded. And here comes the doubt. Now, he's not so sure. "Is Jesus really who He claims to be? Or should we be looking for someone else?" So he sends two of his disciples to Jesus in order to ask Him point blank, as recorded in Luke 7:21 *"Are you the Messiah? Or should we look elsewhere?"*

No where in the Gospel accounts, do we ever read Jesus saying, "What is wrong with this guy? If anybody should know who I am, it should be John!" Does Jesus ever criticize John, or disqualify him from the kingdom of God? Not at all. In fact the Bible tells us in Luke 7:22, *"And Jesus answered and said to them, 'Go back and report to John what you have seen and heard. The blind receive sight. The lame walk. The lepers are cleansed. The deaf hear. The dead are raised up. And the poor have the gospel preached to them'."* Jesus is saying, "Go back and tell John you have seen with your own eyes the evidence. I am the one and only Son of God and he can hold on to that even until death."

So how does this affect Jesus' opinion of John? Does He now think of John as unworthy to serve because of his doubt? After John's disciples leave, Jesus shares with His

Disciples what He thinks of John. Jesus' estimation of John is recorded in Luke 7:28, *"I say to you, among those born of women there is no one greater than John."* John had doubts. Those doubts never minimized John, in the eyes of Jesus.

This is not to say that doubt is something for us to possess and never deal with. God has always sought the kind of relationship with us, that is straightforward and honest. In return, He expects us to seek the same kind of straightforwardness in all of our relationships. But most definitely when it comes to matters of faith. God wants us to be honest about our doubts. Even as we wrestle with the questions we may have, just as John did, we can have confidence that He's not going to turn his back on us.

This is why it is so important for us not to minimize our doubts, but to see them as they really are – a doorway to a deeper closer walk with God. This is the very reason why we need other Believer's, in order to help one another become authentic in our walk with God. Even to the point of letting other people know – "I've got some questions for which I don't have an answer." And to know we won't be looked down upon because of our questions. But that leads to the second step for moving from doubt to faith.

2. Once Identified: Ask God For Help

Here we have to get to what is the source of our doubt? What are we struggling with, specifically? Sit down with God and tell God the truth. Let Him know, (as if He doesn't already), "I'm having a tough time with _______." And then fill in the blank.

One day a father came to Jesus Christ pleading for His help for his son. As this father is asking Jesus to heal his son, Jesus says *"All things are possible to him who believes."* I love what this father said to Jesus, *"I do believe. Help my unbelief."* You know what happened in this situation? Jesus healed his son. Does that sound like any of us? Have we ever found ourselves saying, "I want to God, I really do want to have faith in You, but I'm still wrestling with doubt." It's OK when you're wrestling with questions to go to God and say, "Father, would You strengthen my faith?" Go to God, not as a last resort but as your first step. Get specific with God about your doubt. Be willing to ask God for the wisdom to get answers, to show us the Truth and to open our eyes. Jesus tells us in Matthew 7:7, *"Ask and it will be given to you; seek and you will find; knock and the door will be opened to you. For everyone who asks, receives; and the one who seeks, finds; and to the one who knocks, the door will be opened."*

God isn't offended. He never scolds anyone who says "I don't have this down pat. I need some help." If we seek, God is more than willing to help us find a faith worth holding on to. This is one of the reasons why God wants us connected with other Believers. So we can ask other fellow travelers for help along the way. This fellowship of Believers provides a great source of insight and strength.

We all need places of safety where we can be honest with another person and say, "Everybody seems to believe . . . but I have some doubts." A relationship with others, where no one is going to condemn us. Nobody's going to judge us. They will encourage us and think things through with us. That's what the Christian walk is about.

3. Understand Our Spiritual Journey

The Apostle Paul is certainly a person who understood the struggle we have. If you recall, he was called Saul before he was called Paul. And before becoming a Believer, Saul was a Prosecutor. He saw his mission in life as ridding the world of pesky Christians. And he fulfilled his mission with a passion, imprisoning and even participating in killing Christians.

Then the day came when Paul started his own journey to a faith in Jesus Christ. It's recorded in Acts the ninth chapter. His journey began on the road to Damascus, where God blinds him, sends him to Damascus, where he waits three days with no food or water until Ananias shows up to baptize him. With all that Paul went through to become a Christian, it's no wonder God led him to write in First Corinthians 13:11, *"When I was a child, I used to talk as a child, think as a child, reason as a child; when I became a man, I put aside childish things. At present we see indistinctly, as in a mirror, but then face to face. At present I know partially; then I shall know fully, as I am fully known."*

Struggling with a growing faith is part of our spiritual journey. Just like a child understands things differently as they grow up, so it is true of every Believer. Faith is not an instantaneous event. It is a life long process. In fact I am hearing more and more Believers say, that it's only as they mature in their faith they come to understand how little they know. And all the more reason we need to spend time with others who can nurtured our faith.

Years ago I was a distance runner. (Don't let my lean trim figure fool you.) I loved running. I had raced in a couple of 10 k's runs and noticed that, try as I may, my times were not improving. Even after weeks and months of practice, I was running as slow as I had ever run. One day I was talking with one of the guys from the church about my disappointment and how I wanted to improve my times. And he offered to start running with me. The only problem was – this guy was good. Just keeping up with him on a "light run" was a challenge for me. But as he pushed me each time we ran together, as uncomfortable as that felt, as much as my lungs burned and muscles ached, I was improving. In less than a month my times had improved significantly. I discovered if I kept doing the same thing I had been doing, I was going to get the same results.

I have since discovered this principle is true about our walk with God and matters of faith. I need to be around people who push me. And sometimes push me pretty hard. Do we ever want that kind of thing? No way! Certainly not when it comes to matters of faith. This thing of believing in God and walking with God, ought to be an easy thing – right? But an easy thing is most often a non-growing thing.

If we hang out with people who have a strong, vibrant, passionate and deep faith, we learn from them. They encourage us. They didn't get their faith by accident. They're doing things in their life to build that faith and we can learn from them. Find someone who has the kind of faith you're looking to have and spend some time with them. Buy them a cup of coffee. Just hang out with them and let their life be an influence on your own.

4. Begin A Specific Course Of Action

We are not the first generation to wrestle with faith. Even as the church was beginning, following the Resurrection of Jesus, it took time for people to come to terms with believing what God was saying.

On one occasion Paul and Silas sat down with a group of people in a city called Berea, and shared with them about trusting in this person called Jesus. Acts 17:11, records what the Bereans reaction was to Paul's message: *"The Bereans were eager to hear what Paul and Silas said and studied the Scriptures every day to find out if these things were true. So, many of them believed, as well as many important Greek women and men."*

When the Bereans heard this message from Paul and Silas their reaction was – "Let's get more facts." They set out to study to see if the things they had heard were true. And they focused on the specific evidence regarding what they had heard. This is where we often lose track of overcoming our doubts. We need to get very specific regarding the issue we are struggling with.

Once you identify your specific struggle, figure out what course of action you're going to follow to face your doubt. Don't let the issue be some kind of vague question that kind of swirls around in your mind. You'll never get answers that way. Sit down, take a piece of paper, write a list: "These are my specific questions that I have about Christianity."

The more specific we are in our questions, the more specific God will supply an answer from His Word. And as we get one answer upon another, each will begin to build a bridge to a genuine-lasting faith. Just as the people in Berea found answers to their questions, eventually leading them to faith, so the same can happen in the 21st Century.

5. Test Our Answers

Once we start getting answers, we need to insure those answers are leading us on the right path. The Bible is very clear regarding this. In I John 4:1 we read, *"Beloved, do not believe every spirit, but test the spirits to see whether they are from God; for many false prophets have gone out into the world."*

What does that mean? What is God after? Basically, take our time, investigate what we are learning. Just because we hear someone on the radio, even from a church pulpit, or read a Christian book, all those things need to be tested. And they can be tested in three ways:

A. The Bible

The Bible serves as the standard for every Believer today. It is the "measuring stick" to all matters of faith. The Apostle Paul understood the value of testing, even well intentioned people. He measured himself and every other Apostle and Believer to the same standard – The Bible. Notice what he writes in I Thessalonians 2:13,: *"We also constantly give thanks to God for this, that when you received the word of God that you heard from us, you accepted it not as a human word but as what it really is, God's word, which is also at work in you believers."*

We need to measure what we hear and read against a source that has proved itself reliable for 2000 years. But that is not the only way of testing what we hear and read. A second standard would be:

B. Godly Counsel

Pulling alongside of people who have been "in the faith" for awhile can be a healthy step. Listening to their insight can bring some much needed balance as we are working through some questions. Again, the Bible says in Proverbs 6:20, *"Young man, obey your father and your mother. Take to heart all of their advice; keep in mind everything they tell you. Every day and all night long their counsel will lead you and save you from harm; when you wake up in the morning, let their instructions guide you into the new day."*

In this case the Bible is talking about listening to those in the faith who can give us much needed insight. There are older Believers we can listen to and seek specific answers to our questions. Building a relationship with someone more "mature" in their faith will bring a great insight to matters of faith.

C. Our Own Acceptance

This may sound a little strange, but hear me out. Somewhere along the way, each of us needs to come to a conclusion about our doubts. The Bible is a solid foundation, Godly counsel can give us insight, but we must make up our mind where we stand.

On one occasion Jesus decided to find out where His Disciples stood regarding who He is and what He is doing. And so He asked His disciples in Matthew16:13: *"Who do people say that the Son of Man is? Some say you are john the Baptist. Others say you are Elijah, replied His disciples . . . He said to them, "But who do you say that I am? And Peter replied, "You are the Christ, the Son of God."*

Now you have to give Peter credit, he made a lot of mistakes about a lot of things, but he was right on target when it came to knowing who Jesus is. Without hesitating Peter's reply is, "You are the Son of God!"

Notice, Jesus was most interested in, "And who do *you* say that I am?" Specifically Jesus is looking for, "What conclusions have you personally come to?" It's not a matter of what our parents believed, what our children believe, or what our best friend believes – all of their faith together won't hold up when you're going through a storm of doubt. God wants to know – "What do you believe?"

Someone once said, "We don't have to know everything to know something." God has been gracious. He's given us exactly what we need to know to carry us through the storms of life. Based on God's Truth, we can follow Jesus Christ and have confidence that our eternity is in heaven with Him. There will be issues we may have to wait a while to find and answer – it will come in time.

Let me close with a story. A story most of us are quite familiar with. The story of Thomas, one of the Disciples of Jesus. We know him today as - *Doubting* Thomas. After the resurrection of Jesus, the Disciples tried to explain to Thomas that they had seen Jesus. They had talked with Jesus and that in fact, He was alive. Thomas' reply was, "Unless I see his hands, unless I touch his side, I will not believe."

It's just like Jesus to take a guy up on that kind of challenge. Sure enough, just a day later Jesus meets up with the disciples. This time Thomas is there as well and Jesus comes to Thomas and says – only to Thomas, "Touch my hands, place your hand in my side." Do you remember the response of Thomas? John 20:28 tells us he fell to his knees, without ever touching Jesus and said, *"My Lord and my God!"*

Then and there his faith was driven deep into his soul, by having personally checked out the evidence of the resurrection, so deep that Thomas spent the rest of his life declaring that reality, that Jesus was the one and only Son of God. Eventually, history tells us, Thomas was killed because of his unwillingness to let go of his faith in Jesus Christ.

Wrestling with doubt is something every Believer will have to deal with somewhere along the way. Let's never allow doubt to keep us from having a genuine authentic walk with God. He looks forward to those walks together, where just the two of you can talk about what's on your mind.

Chapter Seven

Conclusions

.

Facts and evidence will only take us so far in our spiritual journey. This may be the reason Jesus taught in Matthew 11:15, *"He who has ears, let him hear."* The question boils down to, "What am I looking for?" More often than not, what we are looking for, has been evident all the time. Someone once said, "No one will ever be argued into the Christian faith. Because it's not just a decision of the mind, it's a decision of the heart." God doesn't want blind faith, neither does He want to see intellectual acceptance of historic fact. He wants to change us, to give us a hope and a future. And that's all found in the person of Jesus Christ.

There was a group of people who seemed to always have a problem with Jesus and His teachings, we refer to them as the Pharisees, the religious leaders of Israel. They had heard what His Disciples had heard. They had seen what His Disciples had seen. But, they remained unmoved, unchanged, unwilling to say Jesus just might be, the Son of God.

They always had themselves elevated above the tax collectors and sinners that were drawn to Jesus. One day Jesus taught a Parable. One of His favorite ways to bring a spiritual point to light. He told the Parable of the Prodigal Son. You may remember the Parable.

It's about a son who goes to his father, asking for his inheritance in advance, then goes to a distant land, wastes all his money and has to start eating with the pigs to survive. The day comes when he *"comes to his senses",* sees the foolishness of his ways and decides to go home to his father. Deciding on his way back home, that he will ask his father for forgiveness and he will live out his days as a servant in his father's house.

We may make the mistake, as some of the Pharisees probably did, that the Parable was about a wayward son. But it's not. The Parable is about the Father. Specifically about the Father's willingness, even though He was entitled to reprimand the son for his foolishness, the willingness of the Father to embrace his son and welcome him home. The heart of the Father is revealed in that part of the Parable that reads, *"But while he (the son) was still a long way off, his father saw him and was filled with compassion for him; he ran to his son, threw his arms around him and kissed him."*

Jesus lets us in on a secret. Our Father in Heaven is watching for us. He checks on us every day, hoping to see that moment when we have "come to our senses" and said enough is enough. It's a moment when all the evidence we have looked at helps, but it's not enough. Because just as the Prodigal son had no good reason to expect his father to accept him back in the family, we too know that going to our Father is not an intellectual effort. We are way out of our league when it comes to matching wits with our

Creator. No, it has to be something more than intellectual acceptance of historic fact. And we would be right.

God is looking for a relationship to be restored. The kind of relationship that was demonstrated way back in the Garden of Eden. When God would come "in the cool of the day" and just walk and talk with Adam and Eve. The very reason we were created in the first place, to walk with God.

Our rebellious hearts separated us from God. He didn't pull away from us, we pulled away from Him. Grandpa Adam and Grandma Eve in essence said, "We can do it on our own." And we've been living that way ever since. But the Parable, reveals a Truth. God is hoping, God is waiting for us to come home. Back to a walk that is truly fulfilling.

Many times we are so consumed with making a living, that we have failed to make a life. This is what Jesus was getting to when He said in John 10:10, *"I have come that they may have life, and have it to the fullest."* And all the evidence we will ever read, all points us to a Father who wants to give us a life that's worth living.

Perhaps what we have looked at together over these few pages has brought you to a point of taking God up on His invitation. It begins with a prayer, just a conversation with God. We don't need to be in a special building, don't have to be with a special person to ask God to forgive us and help us to walk right before Him again. Now there's a lot more involved in becoming a Christian, but that's a great place to begin. If, you're willing to start there, you may want to talk with a pastor or someone you know who can help you discover for yourself the journey of becoming a Follower of Jesus Christ.

Perhaps you are a Believer already. And the evidence we've looked at has helped you in coming to terms with your reasons for believing. Don't slow down! Share what you have with someone. You don't have to know everything in order to share something. Start where you are and let God take you from here to where He wants you to be.

God is not finished with any of us yet. The journey is just beginning.

Appendix

Prophecies & Their Fulfillment Regarding The Messiah

A. *Described as:*

Seed of woman	Gen. 3:15
Promised seed	Gen. 12:1–3; Gal. 3:16
Star out of Jacob	Num. 24:17; Luke 3:34
Of Judah's tribe	Gen. 49:10; Heb. 7:14
Son of David	Isa. 11:1–10; Matt. 1:1
Prophet	Deut. 18:15; Acts 3:22, 23
Priest - Melchizedek's order	Psa. 110:4; Heb. 6:20
King of David's line	Jer. 23:5; Luke 1:32, 33
Son of God	Psa. 2:7, 8; Acts 13:33
Son of Man	Dan. 7:13; Mark 8:38
Immanuel	Isa. 7:14; Matt. 1:22, 23
Branch	Jer. 23:5; Zech. 3:8
Headstone	Psa. 118:22; 1 Pet. 2:4, 7

Servant	Isa. 42:1–4; Matt.12:18, 21

B. *Mission of, to:*

Introduce the new covenant	Jer. 31:31–34; Matt. 26:26–30
Preach the Gospel	Isa. 61:1–3; Luke 4:17–19
Bring peace	Isa. 9:6, 7; Heb. 2:14–16
Die for man's sin	Isa. 53:4–6; 1 Pet. 1:18–20
Unite God's people	Isa. 19:23–25; Eph. 2:11–22
Call the Gentiles	Isa. 11:10; Rom. 15:9–12
Rule from David's throne	Psa. 45:5–7; Acts 2:30–36
Be a priest	Zech. 6:12, 13; Heb. 1:3; 8:1
Destroy Satan	Rom. 16:20; 1 John 3:8
Bring everlasting righteousness	Dan. 9:24; Matt. 3:15; 2 Cor. 5:21

C. *Christ the true Messiah, proved by:*

Birth at Bethlehem	Mic. 5:2; Luke 2:4–7

Born of a virgin	Isa. 7:14; Matt. 1:18–25
Appearing in the 2nd Temple	Hag. 2:7, 9; John 18:20
Working miracles	Isa. 35:5, 6; Matt. 11:4, 5
Vicarious death	Isa. 53:1–12; 1 Pet. 3:18
Coming at the appointed time	Dan. 9:24–27; Mark 1:15

D. *Other prophecies concerning:*

Worship	Psa. 72:10–15; Matt. 2:1–11
Flight to Egypt	Hos. 11:1; Matt. 2:13–15
Forerunner	Mal. 3:1; Mark 1:1–8
Zeal	Psa. 69:9; John 2:17
Triumphal entry	Zech. 9:9, 10; Matt. 21:1–11
Betrayal	Psa. 41:9; Mark 14:10
Being sold	Zech. 11:12; Matt. 26:15
Silent defense	Isa. 53:7; Matt. 26:62
Being spit on	Isa. 50:6; Mark 14:65

Being crucified with sinners	Isa. 53:12; Matt. 27:38
Piercing of hands and feet	Psa. 22:16; John 19:36, 37
Being mocked	Psa. 22:6–8; Matt. 27:39–44
Dying drink	Psa. 69:21; John 19:29
Side pierced	Zech. 12:10; John 19:34
Prayer for the enemies	Psa. 109:4; Luke 23:34
Garments gambled for	Psa. 22:18; Mark 15:24
Death without broken bones	Psa. 34:20; John 19:33
Separation from God	Psa. 22:1; Matt. 27:46
Burial with the rich	Isa. 53:9; Matt. 27:57–60
Preservation from decay	Psa.16:8–10; Acts 2:31
Ascension	Psa. 68:18; Eph. 4:8–10
Exaltation	Psa. 2:6–12; Phil. 2:9, 10

www.ingramcontent.com/pod-product-compliance
Lightning Source LLC
Chambersburg PA
CBHW022158080426
42734CB00006B/484